Depression and Suicide

IN CHILDREN AND ADOLESCENTS

Nina Jo Muse

pro·ed
8700 Shoal Creek Boulevard
Austin, Texas 78758

Printed in the United States of America

pro·ed
8700 Shoal Creek Boulevard
Austin, Texas 78758

10 9 8 7 6 5 4 3 2 1 90 91 92 93 94

Contents

Preface

THE CHILD GUIDANCE MENTAL HEALTH SERIES is the culmination of a cooperative effort by many people who are concerned about a number of mental health issues confronting our children and adolescents. We can no longer afford to believe that childhood is always a carefree, happy time, free of stress and emotional conflict. According to our most reliable sources, approximately 11% of all school-age children (6 to 8 million) are in need of some form of mental health intervention, yet less than half of these receive any form of treatment (Gilmore, Chang, & Coron, 1984, cited in Saxe, Cross, & Silverman, 1988). That is the bad news.

The good news is that experts now agree that treatment for children with emotional/behavioral difficulties can be effective when it is based upon a cooperative effort involving parents, teachers, and mental health professionals. We cannot take a child from a disturbed system, attempt to fix the child, place the child back into the unchanged system, and call it satisfactory treatment. It won't work. We can, however, forge personal liaisons across systems and work together to help our children and adolescents who are both troubled and troubling.

This series is written for parents, teachers, and others who are interested in forging such partnerships to better understand and help our youth. Specific topics were selected due to their impact on today's children and their families. These topics include attention deficit disorder, depression and suicide, and conduct disorders. For each topic, the authors describe (a) the significance and/or impact of the problem, (b) how parents and teachers can recognize the problem, and (c) what to do about it or where to seek help.

The Child Guidance Mental Health Series was commissioned by the Austin Child Guidance Center and funded by the Donald D. Hammill Foundation of Austin, Texas. The authors have donated the proceeds to the Child

Guidance Center, which is a nonprofit outpatient clinic providing mental health services to children and their families in central Texas. All of the authors work full-time in children's services and therefore wrote these books in their "spare" time. A special thanks to each of these generous professionals: Erin Bigler, Nina Jo Muse, Nancy Nussbaum, and Michele Toth. We are also indebted to the Donald D. Hammill Foundation and to PRO-ED, Inc., without whose support we never would have had the courage to attempt this project. Last, I would like to thank June Martinez for her technical assistance in preparing the manuscripts for publication and Donald Zappone, executive director of the Austin Child Guidance Center, for his encouragement.

This series is dedicated to the staff of the Austin Child Guidance Center and to professionals everywhere who commit themselves to helping children.

Maggie Coleman
Series editor
Past president, Board of Directors
Austin Child Guidance Center

CHAPTER 1

What Is Depression?

ONLY IN THE PAST FEW YEARS have mental health professionals recognized that depression and suicide are not the exclusive domain of adults; children and adolescents may also suffer from depression and attempt suicide. Because depression causes the afflicted child much inner turmoil, makes coping with everyday life difficult, and may lead to a dysfunctional adulthood, its prompt recognition and treatment are essential. The following topics are addressed:

- How significant is the problem of depression and suicide in young people?
- What is depression and who gets depressed?
- What are the general signs and symptoms of depression?
- What are the signs and symptoms of depression in youth?
- How can children at risk be identified?
- What are the facts, signs, and symptoms of suicidal behavior?
- What can parents and professionals do?

If we can better understand depression and familiarize ourselves with the risks, signs, and symptoms, we are then in a position to begin helping these young people toward a more promising future.

Contrary to previously held assumptions, depression does occur in children and adolescents. Commonly held beliefs about depression in the under-18 age group are explored in this chapter. Definitions of depression are discussed, and its causes and who it afflicts are examined.

Examples of Depressed Children

"Bobby" is 10 and his parents are concerned about him because his teachers say that he picks on the other children in his class and is not performing to his potential. His early history is unremarkable except for a broken wrist suffered in a fall from a jungle gym at age 5. Bobby's father has a serious, chronic illness.

"Tiffany" is 3 and is discovered in her mother's room eating pills from a pill bottle on the floor. Her mother is on the bed semicomatose from a suicide attempt with the same pills. After both are treated and released in good physical condition from the local emergency room, the mother continues in therapy on a weekly basis with her psychiatrist who urges her to keep her prescription medications out of her child's reach.

"Frank" is 14 and, although quite bright, is flunking four subjects at school. His mother and new stepfather worry that he is quite passive when confronted and freely admits to trying drugs. Last week his teachers noted that he fell asleep in his first period class and seemed drunk. His parents took him home and let him sleep it off. Frank's father, whom he "never got along with," died when Frank was 6.

"Missy" is 15 and has chronic headaches. She makes good grades and comes from a well-respected upper middle class family who attends a fundamentalist church. Her younger sister is now in residential treatment for behavioral problems, but prior to her placement the family had been under enormous stress. Her parents were somewhat mortified at having a family member in psychiatric treatment, but they are very proud of their older daughter.

What do each of the above vignettes have in common? They each appear to describe fairly common problems found in childhood and adolescence: peer problems in a school-age child, ingestion of a nonfood substance by a toddler, poor school performance and drug abuse by a teenage boy, and a chronic physical problem in a teenage girl. In fact, they each have something much more important in common: Each is a composite description of a child with serious depression similar to one who presented to me in my practice as a child psychiatrist. None of the actual patients were described as depressed by their parents or teachers or even their regular doctors. And none of them were described as suicidal, although the first three vignettes contain descriptions of actual suicide attempts.

If these stories did not immediately make you think of depression and suicide, you are in good company. Until quite recently even professionals in the field of mental health did not believe that children under the age of 12 could get depressed, much less attempt suicide. Depression in children was barely mentioned in standard textbooks in psychiatry until the mid-1970s, and although it was recognized that adolescents do get depressed and commit suicide, child/adolescent depression still is largely underdiagnosed. Thousands of children and adolescents in this country suffer needlessly from a treatable condition.

Why Depression Should Cause Concern

In addition to the inner suffering depression causes, it can cause death at any age, either indirectly as a result of withdrawal from the world (e.g., wasting away and starving to death in very severe cases) or directly through suicide. As it is now known that depression in various forms can manifest itself from infancy onward, aggressive treatment is indicated to prevent this lethal outcome. But death is only the most severe outcome. Left untreated, depressed children and adolescents have been shown to have problems in school, difficulty making and keeping friends, and trouble getting along with their parents and siblings. More severe problems can also result, such as alcohol and drug abuse, and other conduct and behavioral disorders.

It is the purpose of this book to dispel the myths surrounding depression and suicide in the under-18 age group. The book is also intended to help parents and teachers recognize symptoms and patterns in children and their families that may indicate the presence of depression and the spectre of suicide. If we can recognize the problem, we are in a position to take appropriate action to alleviate it. First, however we must clear our minds of dangerous myths.

The Myths

1. Children do not get depressed.
   Fact: It is estimated by experts that 4% to 8% of all youngsters are significantly depressed.

2. Children do not kill themselves.
   Fact: In 1985, 278 children under 15 are known to have committed suicide, and 5,121 adolescents killed themselves that year (National Center for Health Statistics, 1988).

3. Childhood is a special time without cares or worries.
   Fact: Children experience stress, anxiety, and emotional upset at rates comparable to adults.

4. Children have no concept of death.
Fact: By age 7 most children have a fairly realistic concept of death.

5. Depression is an excuse used by the weak.
Fact: No one chooses to be depressed. Many depressions have biological components over which the person has no control.

6. Some children are just accident prone.
Fact: Frequent accidents may indicate depression, suicidal wishes, or a medical problem.

7. Depression in children is just another phase and will get better with time.
Fact: Untreated depression tends to recur repeatedly throughout a person's life and can lead to drug abuse, behavioral problems, and suicide.

8. Talk of suicide is just an attempt to get attention and manipulate others.
Fact: Children who threaten suicide are depressed and/or know of no other means to get the help they need.

9. Children don't need to go to psychiatrists/psychologists.
Fact: Many psychiatrists and psychologists specialize in children. Child psychiatrists are the most in-demand medical specialists in the country.

10. Children are not affected deeply by what happens to them. They bounce back.
Fact: Although children are quite adaptable if supported, trauma during the period of development prior to adulthood is more likely to have serious consequences than trauma that occurs after maturity. However, these consequences may not be obvious until adulthood.

Definitions of Depression

This section defines depression, outlines its causes, and describes people who are most at risk to develop it.

What Is Depression?

Before proceeding further, it will be advantageous to delineate our subject more clearly. Just what is depression? *Webster's New World Dictionary* (1988) states that depression is "an emotional condition, either neurotic or psychotic, characterized by feelings of hopelessness, inadequacy, etc." As used by professionals in the field of mental health, depression as an illness refers to a syndrome of abnormally dejected mood persistent over time that interferes with daily living. It does not refer to normal feelings of sadness after the loss of a loved person or object. It does not refer to the normal feelings of disappointment when events in our lives go contrary to our desires. All of us, adults and children alike, feel depressed at various times in our lives, but not all of us experience depression—the illness.

Depression as an illness is not a disease in the usual sense of the word; rather, it is a syndrome. It is a collection of symptoms reported by the person involved and signs observable by others. These symptoms and signs form a pattern recognizable by professionals and others trained to see it. Of course, the major symptom is a depressed mood—an emotional state of low spirits, dejected feelings, sadness, and unhappiness persistent over time and out of proportion to life events. This mood change is accompanied by a variable number of changes in other life spheres such as enjoyment of activities, appetite and/or weight, sleep, activity level, energy level, self-esteem, concentration, and future orientation.

What Causes Depression?

The changes described cannot be attributed to a recognized physical illness, but professionals now believe that there may be a physical cause to many depressions. For example, it is known that significant depression can run in families, leading researchers to propose a genetic or hereditary basis. Depressed people may show changes on some blood tests; although this does not prove a biological cause, it does show that some depression is not entirely psychological.

A few years ago, two main types of depression were recognized: endogenous and exogenous. Supposedly, the endogenous type arose from within the person and was not necessarily related to life events and circumstances. This type was later theorized to be of biological or physical origin. Exogenous depression was supposedly engendered by life stresses such as the death of a loved one, loss of a job, or pressure to succeed. In these cases it was thought that the person did not bounce back as he or she should have from the ordinary or maybe even extraordinary losses and problems in life. Each type of depression theoretically had slightly different signs and symptoms. In actuality, it was frequently hard to distinguish between these two types of depression.

Other purely psychological theories of depression postulate that some individuals feel bad because their consciences are punishing them for real or imagined wrongs they have committed. These people become depressed because their conscience (or "superego" in psychological terms) is too rigid and harsh. It demands perfection of them, which is, of course, impossible to attain. Another theory holds that depression is the result of holding anger and rage inside instead of finding a healthy outlet for it. Instead of venting their anger upon the environment, these people theoretically turn it upon themselves and so are miserable and depressed. In extreme cases it is felt that the anger at the self becomes so intense that suicide is attempted.

Who Gets Depressed?

Current thinking postulates that certain people inherit a predisposition to some type of depression, and under stress this tendency may develop into illness. Some people are therefore relatively prone to depression, and some people are relatively resistant to it. Probably, anyone can become seriously depressed if subjected to enough stress over a long enough period of time. It is also possible that over time, certain kinds of stress can induce physical or biological changes in the body and cause depression. This idea is supported by the fact that some medicines can cause depression.

The important thing to remember from this discussion is that the illness of depression is not "all in one's head." Just as one is not able to will away asthma through positive thinking, depressed people cannot will away their depression. This is not to negate the fact that depressed people, including children, sometimes get better even without specific treatment. Depression is notorious for its fluctuating course, its characteristic ups and downs. Depression is frequently a cyclic illness with many remissions and exacerbations along its natural untreated course. Unfortunately, this characteristic can fool us into not taking the illness seriously.

As you read about the characteristics of depression, keep in mind that the definitions and descriptions apply equally to adults. In addition to children you know, you may recognize a friend, coworker, or even yourself on these pages. It is estimated that in any given year, somewhat more than 5% of the entire adult population experiences a significant depression (Earls, 1984). Over a lifetime it is estimated that about 25% of all adults will experience a significant depression (Earls, 1984). Children probably suffer from depression at a lower but still alarming rate. Recent studies show that perhaps as many as 8% of all adolescents are depressed, and perhaps almost 2% of younger children are depressed (Kashani et al., 1987). This translates into an enormous amount of human suffering that is potentially treatable.

CHAPTER 2

How Do We Recognize Depression?

THIS CHAPTER INCLUDES A LISTING of the various behaviors that may be affected in a depressed individual. Then these same signs and symptoms are discussed relative specifically to children and adolescents.

SIGNS AND SYMPTOMS OF DEPRESSION

To begin to see the depressed individuals in our midst, let's look more closely at the behavior changes accompanying depressed mood. These behavior changes can be noted in such areas as eating and sleeping habits, energy level, ability to concentrate, self-esteem, enjoyment of life, and attitude toward the future.

Enjoyment of Activities

Depressed people in general (children, adolescents, and adults) can lose interest in activities they usually enjoy. Nothing is particularly fun for them anymore. Often they just don't seem to want to do anything.

Appetite/Weight

Depressed persons may begin to eat a lot less than they used to—or a lot more. Consequently, they may lose a lot of weight—or gain a lot of weight. Just what is a lot? Anything gained or lost in excess of 5% of the original body weight is considered significant. For example, a 100-pound person who loses 6 pounds in a few weeks has lost more than 5% of his or her body weight. For this to be meaningful, of course, the person must not have been consciously trying to lose weight. If a person whom most people would not consider overweight diets and loses significant amounts of weight, this may also indicate a serious mental health problem, although not necessarily depression. In children and adolescents some appetite and weight changes are a normal part of growth and development, so this must be taken into account.

Sleep

Depressed people tend to have very characteristic changes in their sleeping patterns. Usually they sleep less (insomnia). More rarely, they sleep more hours per night than previously (hypersomnia). Insomnia comes in several varieties. There is trouble getting to sleep (initial insomnia), trouble staying asleep (frequent awakening), and early morning awakening with failure to return to sleep (terminal insomnia). The first, initial insomnia, is common in all of us when anxious or worried. The other two, frequent awakening and terminal insomnia, are more characteristic of depression. Typically, in depressed persons the total amount of sleep time per night is decreased. This can lead to problems in the next category.

Energy Level/Activity Level

Depressed people frequently complain that they are tired all the time and have no energy. Examination by a physician will usually reveal no physical cause. Other depressed people may notice that they actually move more slowly and look tired or run down. In extreme cases, depressed persons may actually refuse to get out of bed and engage in their usual daily routine. They may talk more slowly, walk more slowly, do simple household tasks more slowly, and their thinking may be slowed down. Occasionally, depressed people may appear very agitated and nervous. They may appear to do things rapidly, but the total time it takes them to accomplish tasks is actually increased.

Concentration

Whether depressed persons appear "slowed down" or "speeded up" due to agitation, their mental processes are almost always slowed down. This is because they are unable to concentrate as well as they previously did. Some people may complain of inability to concentrate or that their memory is just not working. Family and friends may notice that depressed persons have trouble making decisions or take inordinate amounts of time to answer simple questions. They may indeed begin to forget appointments or things they were supposed to accomplish.

Self-Esteem

Depressed people often complain of not feeling good about themselves, of being responsible for the bad things that happen in their families even if this is obviously not the case. They worry sometimes of being "found out," that although they are successful at least outwardly in life, they do not deserve the success. They feel as if they are imposters and someone else is going to discover it. Others may notice that they are extremely uncomfortable with compliments and do not know how to respond to them. They may not stand up for themselves when challenged. They may also avoid roles of leadership and avoid doing new things or doing things spontaneously.

Future Orientation

Typically, depressed persons feel that the future is bleak. They tend to worry more about the future than necessary, and this blinds them to the positive aspects of the present. They may think of death either in passive terms, such as wishing they had never been born, or in more active terms, such as planning various ways to kill themselves. Observers may notice that they talk a lot about illnesses, that they never talk hopefully of the future, or that they speak of suicide.

What to Look for in Young People

Did these descriptions of the behavior changes accompanying depression remind you of anyone you know? Did it remind you of any children you know? It is much more likely that the above descriptions reminded you of an adult or adolescent than a child, and herein lies the problem of recognizing depression in children. Each section above describes what a depressed person might complain of (symptoms), along with what other people can actually observe (signs). Children and adolescents are not particularly good at identifying their sources of distress, giving them labels, and then communicating this in words to the adults in their lives. Even if they do recognize that something is wrong and give it an appropriate label, such as "I feel like dying" or "I don't sleep very well," they are not apt to spontaneously report this to their teachers and parents. In other words, they do not as a general rule complain of *symptoms.* This, however, does not mean that they are incapable of talking about how they feel and what is going on in their lives. Children and adolescents may manifest depression in different ways than adults. This section is devoted to helping adults recognize the indirect ways in which young people may indicate they are depressed.

If children don't complain of symptoms, what do they do? How can we tell if something is wrong? Fortunately, there are many clues. Children may not talk about their symptoms, but they do act them out. They exhibit the *signs* of depression that any observer can verify with his or her own eyes. If this is true, then why is it so hard for all of us to see the depressed children in our midst? It is hard because of the myths mentioned before and because we tend to attribute the behaviors that children exhibit as just a phase they are going through, as misbehavior, or as manipulation. We often do not take what children do or say seriously. If they say something unexpected such as, "I want to kill myself!" in the middle of an argument, we pass it off as manipulation or an unintended remark hurled in anger. We *assume* we know what is going on, and then we do something even more deplorable. We don't *ask* the child what *is* going on! In other words, we often see what we want to see or what we have been conditioned to see by our own upbringing. The reasons the symptoms and signs of depression go largely unnoticed in children and adolescents can be summarized as follows:

1. Children have trouble identifying and verbalizing feelings and sources of distress.
2. Children usually do not talk spontaneously about their problems.
3. Adults frequently discount the importance of what children say and do.
4. Adults usually assume they already know what is going on with children.
5. Adults often fail to ask children about their feelings and behavior.

Fortunately, we can learn to look at our children with fresh eyes and learn to read the signs of distress that their behavior communicates. With this in mind, let us go back over the list of changes accompanying depressed mood and make the descriptions more detailed and specific to children.

Enjoyment of Activities

We know that depressed children, like depressed adults, may lose interest in previously enjoyed activities, but how does this translate into observable behavior? What do we look for? If Derek used to love to go to his scouting meetings and now he does not want to go, this may signal a problem. However, it may be more subtle than this. Maybe Derek used to come bouncing in from his meetings bursting to tell Mom or Dad what happened, and now he has nothing to say about them. Maybe the problem is not depression but rather a change in scout masters, but to find out we must ask questions.

Distressed children may gradually withdraw from activities that are not initiated by parents. They may first give up those activities that involve several peers, such as scouting, after-school soccer, or dance lessons. More severely distressed children may avoid activities that involve just one peer. They may not instigate play with a friend anymore, may quit inviting friends over to play or stay the night, may quit accepting invitations from friends to go to their homes, may lose interest in friends altogether, or may not have any friends.

Severely depressed children may even give up activities generally enjoyed alone, such as stamp collecting, drawing pictures, watching TV, or reading. There may be other reasons for giving up activities such as these, but to find out we must ask the child.

A child may not actively avoid or give up activities, but parents or teachers may notice that he or she complains that everything is "boring" or "stupid." There may be complaints that all the kids are "mean" or "stupid" or "don't like me." When not in school or engaging in scheduled activities, the child may just stay in his or her room.

Although these instances do not necessarily mean that a child is unequivocably depressed, problems may exist that need investigation.

Appetite/Weight

Children go through normal periods of lessened appetite and decreased rate of growth; however, as a general rule they do not lose weight or stay at exactly the same weight for long periods of time until after puberty. Obviously, obese children are able to lose weight through conscious dieting just as adults are, but we are concerned with weight loss that is not intentional. If you are concerned that your child is not growing appropriately, growth charts are available through your local physician that can help determine if his or her growth is appropriate.

As a general rule, weight loss with depression in children is less common than it is in adolescents and adults. When depressed for a long period of time, children tend more often to gain weight inappropriately. But children who are depressed because of serious losses in the recent past may eat less and consequently lose weight. Also, children do not state that they are not as hungry as they used to be. They are more likely to state that they do not like what you have made or that it tastes bad if their appetite is decreased. They may suddenly crave sweets and refuse nutritious food that they have previously enjoyed.

Food is one of the most consistently gratifying and readily available means to make oneself feel good. This is why, over the long haul, I have seen more obese depressed children than underweight ones. Adults in the same situation have options available to them for instant gratification other than food (e.g., drugs, alcohol, sex, fast cars, spending money). The housewife who goes shopping when feeling "blue" may be a stereotype, but shopping *is* one of the common methods that adults use to console themselves. Although young children do not usually have access to these methods, adolescents do and they may indulge in any or all of the ones listed.

Sleep

Children do experience changes in sleep patterns as a result of depressed mood; however, parents and teachers are generally not aware that this is causing a child's sudden refusal to get up in the morning or sleepiness during class. Children may appear to be daydreaming more at school or to not be concentrating as well on their studies, or they may appear more forgetful than previously. Some adults may interpret the change in behavior as a result of interrupted sleep as "laziness" or obstinacy on the child's part. The children themselves may not be aware of the interrupted sleep, just that they feel very tired in the morning. However, when depressed, children may complain of nightmares, or the parent may be awakened in the night by a fearful child. Nightmares can be a result of anxiety and tension experienced along with the depression. Children who regularly sleep less than 7 to 8 hours a night probably should be asked about their sleep and checked by the family doctor.

Alternatively, sleeping all the time may signal depression. The adolescent who is always asleep in his or her room may have a serious problem. Sleep is a good way to avoid an unpleasant life or the sad mood that accompanies depression. It can become a form of escape from emotional pain. Regularly sleeping longer than 8 to 9 hours per night may indicate a medical or emotional problem.

Energy/Activity Level

Classically, depression results in a subjective feeling of tiredness and a lowered level of activity, although anxious depressed children and adults can appear quite "hyper." Depression can be one of the reasons for hyperactivity in the classroom, which should be considered in any child displaying this behavior. At home the behavior may not be particularly noticeable. The increased activity level may manifest as inability to finish projects that the child starts because of being distracted by something else. It may manifest as accident-proneness or carelessness in tasks. The child may seem willfully disobedient of house or school rules. The anxious depressed child may be the one who is into every activity imaginable, but not doing particularly well at any of them. He or she may be very glib and seem not to take anything very seriously. The depressed child may be the class clown.

Children who complain of being tired or bored all the time may be depressed. These children with decreased energy and lowered activity level may not be performing to their ability in school, much to the perplexity of teachers and parents. These children may not act out at all and seem to be concentrating well at school, and yet for some reason they always forget their homework assignments. These may be the children who do everything slowly, dawdling on the way home from school, taking interminable amounts of time getting dressed in the morning, or always being late. These behaviors can also be related to changes in concentration.

Concentration

When a child cannot concentrate, what do we see? Perhaps, we see a child who has difficulty following simple instructions, or who cannot finish anything, or who makes many careless mistakes. The daydreamer in class may be showing signs of decreased concentration and depression. Children who interrupt or who demand help with everything may not be able to concentrate as well as they used to. Again, these may be the children who are always forgetting something they should have remembered—their lunch, their homework, to take out the trash, their best friend's birthday party. These children may think that they are stupid and complain of not being able to do anything right. Unwittingly, exasperated parents can reinforce this notion so that the child becomes entrenched in a negative self-fulfilling prophecy and further depression. This could be the child who responds "Huh?" to every question, necessitating that the teacher repeat it.

This child may *appear* to be concentrating well. There Debbie sits reading her book very attentively. She has not gotten up from the chair once in the past 15 minutes—she has not even looked up. However, Debbie has not managed to complete even a single page. When she reads out loud in class, she may misread words, or start the same line twice, or ask for help as to which line the class is on. Sometimes problems such as these are the result of specific developmental reading disorders, but when they appear in a previously good reader, it may be that concentration is impaired and depression is the cause.

Children who have difficulty concentrating may be able to stay on task for long periods of time but fail to get anything accomplished. Bobby set out to clean up his room a half hour ago, and although he has been diligently working in his room, it does not look much different from when he started. Organizational skills are sometimes difficult for the depressed child to muster.

Self-Esteem

The self-esteem of children and how to encourage a positive self-image has become a popular topic in the press. What signs indicate that there is a problem in this area? Poor self-esteem may appear on the surface as shyness—the child who hangs back when others are eager to try new things. Tiffany is a very musical child but is reluctant to be in the choir, although her teacher and parents have encouraged her. Josh refuses to try out for any sports that require demonstrating aptitude in front of his peers, although his coordination and physical skills are excellent. This is even more puzzling in view of the fact that when forced to try out in the past, he has always made the team and immensely enjoyed playing on it.

Poor self-esteem may be very obvious as in children who repeatedly make negative statements about themselves. Jennifer made an 84 on her last math test when she usually makes in the 90s. She told her mother, "I'm stupid! I can't do anything right!" Children with poor self-esteem may become frustrated very easily and not be able to tolerate any setback. They may demand perfection of themselves, because anything less is evidence that the inner poor self-image is correct. Any attempts to tell children that they are all right will meet with frustration and anger. Jennifer's mom tried to console her: "Look, Jenny, all your other marks are in the 90s; this one is not very important." "You don't understand! I'll never get it right! My teacher hates me and the kids will all make fun of me because I always get an A!" The child's inner reality of "I'm bad" or "I'm no good" is much more compelling than a logical discussion of the actual importance of one bad grade.

A corollary of the poor self-image and low self-esteem is the inability to accept compliments. "Why Brooke, how lovely you look in that new dress," says the teacher. "Oh, it's just a hand-me-down from my sister. It's not even the right length," explains Brooke, instead of just saying thank you with a smile. Children with flagging self-esteem may also be reluctant to take on the compliment of added responsibilities given to them by a parent or teacher.

Instead of pursuing perfection as an antidote to the feelings of unworthiness within, children may go to the opposite extreme. (For example, if they are bad enough, at least the inside and the outside will match up. They are not any good, so why try to be good? It's a hopeless task, after all.) Zachary plays havoc with his fourth-grade class and teacher. He is always taking a pencil that is not his, terrorizing a timid second grader, or mouthing off to the teacher. It seems that he works at getting caught—he seems almost relieved when punished, only to start another maddening round of pranks and misbehavior the next day.

Meet Mallory, the girl who gives everything away. If you're 8 and admire her new hair clip, she's apt to give it to you. She follows all the other third-grade girls around the playground, but nobody is really her friend. She likes to talk to the teacher and bring her things. She's desperate for you to like her because she hates herself. The trouble is, when Mallory is 13, or maybe 12, or even 11, she may give herself away—to any boy or man who will have her. If you ask 13-year-old Mallory how she feels about sex, you'll find that it doesn't even feel good to her.

Future Orientation

We all have our hopes, desires, illusions, maybe even delusions about what the future will bring, and many times this is what gets us through the present. But what if the future looks as bleak or bleaker to us than the present? And what if that present is already very bleak? Never mind that to the casual observer our life looks rather carefree. Maybe we are 9 years old and Mom is busy all the time with our 4-year-old brother who has seizures. He has to go to the doctor a lot, and we must not play roughly with him or get him too upset. Mom is really proud of how we help out with our little brother. Dad just got a great new job and makes a bunch more money than he used to. We have a lot of awesome stuff at home like the swimming pool, VCR, and every electronic toy imaginable. It's too bad we don't get to see Dad very much anymore. That new law firm takes more of his time than even law school did. We get good grades at school, but then Mom and Dad expect that. Why don't we feel so good? We thought everything would be better in the fourth grade. So maybe when Dad thoughtlessly scolds us for being careless at dinner—spilling our milk—we get really upset. Dad tells us we're too big to cry when corrected. We say we hate Dad. Mom yells that we must not think that way, and what a horrible thing that is to say. We say we wish we had never been born and we wish we were dead. Dad says we don't mean that.

But the trouble is the child does mean it, at least part of the time. This is an example of a child who may act on the impulse later if not taken seriously now. Although it is true that children and adolescents frequently do not truly intend to die when carrying out threats of suicide, this does not mean that they may not actually die or at least harm themselves seriously. Children who feel trapped in painful or unpleasant life situations can lose hope for the future and become suicidal. We must remember that how children view their lives may be quite different from what other family members or outsiders see, but it is the child's view that matters if we are to detect the presence of depression and the possibility of suicide. We must look for the clues and ask questions.

Although suicidal ideation and attempts are dramatic examples of how future orientation may change in depression, there are more subtle manifestations of hopelessness about the future. Children who have no dreams, plans, or goals for when they grow up may be seriously depressed. This lack of anticipation may show up as an inability to answer the question, "What do you want to be when you grow up?" or it may show up in a reluctance or inability to prepare in practical ways for the immediate future. Why do homework today if you can't even imagine a tomorrow?

Other Symptoms

The characteristics of hopeless and suicidal children are discussed more thoroughly later in this book. However, in addition to the previously mentioned categories of symptoms and signs of depression, we can look for other clues and changes. One of the most obvious of these clues is the child who looks sad most of the time. Most of us assume we know the face of sadness and despair, but it may be helpful to delineate this more explicitly. A sad expression may consist of a downturned or expressionless mouth, downcast eyes, furrowed brows, a slumped posture, sagging shoulders, and, of course, tearfulness.

Speech may be soft with sparse answers to questions, just a word or two, and lack detail and enthusiasm. There may be little eye contact and no response to attempts at levity. When the child is walking, look for dragging feet, eyes on the ground, sagging shoulders, and a preoccupied attitude.

A previously well child may develop bouts of physical ailments at home or school that foil all attempts at treatment. Good examples of these are recurrent aches and pains including headaches and stomachaches, frequent infections, excessive fatigue, sudden return of bedwetting and/or soiling in a previously well-toilet-trained child, and sudden excessive clumsiness. It is often thought that these symptoms represent symbolic cries for help, but they may be viewed in other ways. When we do not feel well, the little aches and pains of life can loom larger; it can become harder to ignore them. It has been shown by researchers that depressed people have impaired immune function (Kaplan & Sadock, 1985, 1988). This means that their bodies may not fight off viruses and bacteria as efficiently as those of healthy people.

The theory that depression is anger turned inward can be invoked to explain fatigue. It takes an enormous amount of energy to keep overwhelming anger in check, which can lead to great fatigue. This anger could unconsciously be translated into bedwetting and soiling. What would be more upsetting and exasperating to a parent than a child who refuses to control his or her bodily functions? As an expression of anger and a way to get back at grown-ups, it is almost unbeatable. (A word of caution here. Bedwetting and soiling as an expression of anger may not be at all volitional by the child. She or he may be totally unaware of the connection between the feeling and the behavior, and conscious control may not be possible without some type of intervention. In any case, punishment for this type of behavior has been shown to be exceptionally ineffective in eradicating it. Additionally, there are other serious causes for these problems that must be explored before the assumption is made that depression and/or anger are the cause.)

Sudden clumsiness may be the result of fatigue, decreased concentration, the hopelessness accompanying depression, or all three. In the last case, it may mask suicidal thoughts. Sudden clumsiness and accident-proneness may be manifestations of the conscious or unconscious desire to harm the self. There really is no such thing as *just* an accident-prone child; an underlying cause should always be sought. Many incidents that parents, teachers, and even the police interpret as accidents are really intentional acts, halfhearted or even more serious suicide attempts. Careful questioning can help to determine the true nature of these incidents.

Summary

Always look for change as the major clue to the presence of depression in children and adolescents. Any consistent change in a child's behavior in a negative direction should be investigated by parents and teachers whether it occurs suddenly or gradually. Depressed children are not necessarily going to show all of the changes mentioned above, but they are likely to have more than one of them. Some children will have changes in only one or two categories, while other children will have changes in nearly all of them. The most important thing to remember is to look for the changes and then investigate them appropriately. See Appendix A for a summary of the characteristic signs and symptoms of depression.

CHAPTER 3

How Do We Identify Children at Risk?

SOME CHILDREN AND ADOLESCENTS run a higher risk of becoming depressed. In this chapter genetic, physical, familial, and personal history risk factors are outlined.

FAMILY LINKS

So far we have been discussing depressed children and their personal characteristics as clues to the presence of depression. There are other ways of approaching the problem. We can identify children at risk for developing depression by looking at their family situations. Because depression can run in families, the offspring of depressed parents are at risk for depression and such children should be watched for development of behavioral clues. This genetic risk is greatest if one or both parents have had depression, but it is still increased if only an aunt, uncle, or grandparent has the disorder. Beardslee (1984) cites studies that suggest that depressed mothers are not as emotionally available to their children and that this is associated with more emotional problems including depression in their children.

If relatives have other forms of mental, emotional, or behavioral problems, the children may also be at risk for depression. For example, alcoholism and depression have been found to coexist in families, leading some researchers in the mental health field to postulate a connection between alcoholism and depression (Kaplan & Sadock, 1985). The same is also true for other serious mental disorders such as schizophrenia and mania. Our understanding of these disorders and what causes them is so imperfect that it is safe to say that where there is one such problem in a family, it is reasonable to look for others.

Family Stress

Depression may run in families for other than genetic reasons. In addition to a family history of depression and other disorders, we can look for families under significant stress. In the example of alcoholism, children of an alcoholic parent may witness violence, experience physical and/or sexual abuse, or suffer from parental neglect as a result of the alcoholism. All of these stresses could conceivably cause depression, even without a strong genetic component.

Losses

Losses of all kinds including death, divorce, and illness are linked to childhood depression. After the loss of a parent or other close family member through death, it is natural that children feel angry, sad, or depressed for a period of time. If these feelings are not attended to by empathetic adults and the child allowed to go through a healthy grieving process, the feelings can worsen instead of resolving over time. Depression may result. Children with a genetic predisposition to depression will need more support than usual, because it will take less stress from the environment to trigger depression in them than in other children.

Beware of children who have a parent or other very close family member who died by suicide; they are at particular risk for depression and suicide. Suicide is the natural lethal outcome of severe depression. It cannot be overemphasized that suicide is a preventable outcome in most cases if the warning signs are heeded. Children who come from these families are probably at increased genetic risk for depression, but they also experience the devastation such a loss entails. For children, there is increased anger at the person who commits suicide and leaves them, in contrast to the natural anger most children feel for a loved one who dies. This is because children perceive that the person chose death in preference to staying with them. This in turn may increase the natural guilt that most survivors, including children, feel at remaining alive. Children who experience suicide in a close family member will wonder how they have been so bad that the other person wanted to leave them on purpose. The younger the children, the more likely that they will feel that the suicide is their fault. This anger and guilt can fester in an unsupported child and lead to very severe depression and suicidal thoughts.

Many times children will make suicide attempts that are not recognized by others for what they are. For example, children may become accident-prone and constantly be sustaining minor injuries on the playground or at school. Sometimes these children successfully kill themselves when older or even years later as adults. In any case, they are at an increased risk for depression, alcohol and drug abuse, and other behavioral problems. Suicide is such an important issue that it is discussed at length later in this book.

Divorce

Loss of a parent and other family members through divorce is another very painful loss for children. In some ways it is more painful than loss through death. When someone dies, if children are allowed to grieve appropriately and are given support by adults, they come to realize that death is inevitable for all, is irreversible, and had nothing to do with their personal actions. However, in divorce, children perceive that their parents had a choice and therefore could have prevented the divorce. This leads to anger that is harder to work through because it is reality-based. Additionally, because divorce is potentially reversible, children will hold on to the idea of the intact family much longer and have a more difficult time letting go of it. And there is always the suspicion underneath that the child was perhaps responsible for the divorce, which leads to guilt feelings. In fact, children often do play some part in the causes of divorce, albeit an innocent one, but it is this fact that can make guilt particularly difficult to deal with. Anger, unrealistic hope, and guilt feelings that are not resolved are very stressful for children and can lead to a host of problems including depression.

Illness

Illness in a family member is another kind of loss that is stressful for children. It is the loss of the healthy parent or sibling or child himself or herself. For example, an ill parent, especially one with a long chronic illness, cannot attend to a child in the same way that a healthy parent can. The ill parent may not be able to spend as much time with the child, may not be able to physically interact with the child, may not have the energy to interact with the child, or may be preoccupied with himself or herself. A person in pain usually has less patience to deal with a child. Additionally, it is stressful for children to see someone they look to for support and guidance be unable to provide it. The child may perceive that growing up does not have enough rewards to compensate for the things that must be given up along the way. The child may perceive a similar future for himself or herself. All these things are very stressful, and if not dealt with, can lead to problems including depression.

Illness in a sibling can drain off parental time, emotional stamina, and patience and leave the healthy sibling feeling neglected and unimportant. The well child may feel taken for granted and unappreciated as if his or her accomplishments are not as meaningful as those of the ill sibling. This can lead to resentment, anger, and guilt at feeling hateful toward an ill brother or sister. Again, behavioral problems and/or depression can result if the well sibling is not given empathy and adult support.

Even illness in an extended family member such as a grandmother or uncle can result in significant stress for a family and child if the child's daily life is affected in negative ways by that illness. Not to be overlooked is the very real stress of the financial drain of an extended illness on a family. If the parents are stressed in significant ways by the illness of any family member, it can be assumed that the children will also be under stress, even if they have no direct contact or association with the ill person. Children respond to the emotional state of their parents and will reflect that state in their emotions and behavior even if the parents hide or try to hide the stress and its cause.

Finally, illness of a chronic or particularly severe type in children themselves can predispose them to depression. Children with leukemia or other sometimes fatal illnesses can become depressed over their future just as adults with these disorders can. The additional stress of long and/or frequent hospitalizations, with the attendant separations from family and friends, are particularly difficult for children who need the constant support of others even in "well" times. Add to this the pain of necessary operations and routine procedures, and even the most emotionally healthy and well-supported child may become depressed.

Even if an illness is not life-threatening, it can be so stressful as to trigger depression of a serious nature. Congenital problems such as abnormally formed or missing body parts may be tolerated by children until they begin school and have to withstand the stares and ridicule of peers and insensitive adults. With supportive parents and a school environment that encourages all children to explore their potential, these children frequently do well in the primary grades only to founder as adolescence begins. Their perception of themselves as unattractive to the opposite sex as compared to their peers may be particularly difficult to overcome. Adolescence is a time noted for its preoccupation with being like the "in" group, and to children with congenital deformities that affect physical appearance, this may be the most stressful time of their lives. Coupled with the normal moodiness often seen at puberty, these children may just not be able to cope and may succumb to depression of a serious nature.

As you can see, stress in the form of losses can come in many different guises: loss of important people in actual fact through death, loss of people in practical terms through divorce or illness, and loss of the healthy self through illness or disfigurement. These losses are fairly obvious, but there are many others we tend to overlook. There is loss of family and friends through family moves to different cities, states, or even countries. If the chance for contact with previously close persons is limited after the move, these losses can be as stressful as deaths, especially for a child. Loss of a treasured pet through death or other circumstances may be very stressful for a child or even an adult if attachment to the animal was very great. It is a good rule of thumb that the more isolated and solitary the person, the more the death of the pet will affect him or her.

Even the loss of inanimate objects can trigger depression, if the object was very important to the person involved. Children certainly do grieve the loss of their special blankets or other soft toys from infancy if these are removed too soon or precipitously. With support, most children survive these losses without incident, but if this has followed other important losses such as death of a parent, then the child's coping mechanisms may be overcome and the illness of depression may result.

Loss of people, health, animals, objects, and even particular life situations is a necessary and unavoidable part of life. After these losses, it is natural to go through a process of grieving if attachment to these things was great. If this process of grieving is interfered with, cut short, or not nurtured and supported in healthy ways, then depression can result in susceptible individuals. If unnecessary losses are forced upon children for irrational or arbitrary reasons by the adults around them, then depression can also result. Life itself will conspire over time to deprive us of many of the things that we care about; it therefore behooves us to prevent losses for our children when possible.

Other Stresses

The stresses in families leading to depression can be more subtle than those associated with illness and loss of important objects. These less obvious stresses include ones such as illustrated in the vignette in Chapter 2 about the suicidal 9-year-old with a younger brother who has seizures. The stresses in that situation included lack of empathy and emotional support along with the pressure to succeed from ambitious, success-oriented parents. Of course, we have already identified the stress that a chronically ill sibling can cause. Any one of these alone might not have been enough to trigger depression in a child, but if they occur together, a child's coping mechanisms may be overwhelmed.

Other important family stresses that should be considered include financial difficulties, significant change in employment status (e.g., mother returning to work after extended period of homemaking), chronic unemployment or underemployment (especially when affecting the male parent), birth of a sibling, remarriage with addition of stepparents and step-siblings, drug abuse by family members, trouble with the law, family violence, incest, prominence of family in the community (highly visible families can experience more overall stress), and family infighting over property, custody, and so on. Just as the major clue to depression in children is change in previous behaviors and level of functioning, the sine qua non of stress in the family is change in previous patterns of family interaction. Any changes, even for the better, can cause significant levels of stress and therefore distress in family members. If this stress becomes great enough and/or combines with other factors predisposing to illness, depression can result for children and other family members.

CHAPTER 4

Suicide

EVERYONE WHO WORKS WITH CHILDREN and adolescents should be knowledgeable about suicidal behavior. The characteristics of suicide, factors influencing suicidal behavior, and how to recognize such behaviors are presented in this chapter.

The Prevalence of Suicide

Suicide is the intentional ending of one's own life by any means and can be the natural lethal outcome of severe depression. The possibility of suicide is important to consider because it is very serious, relatively common, and is preventable if the warning signs are identified and taken seriously. Most people, including children and adolescents, give ample warning that an attempt is impending if only we will listen to their direct and indirect cries for help. If the possibility of suicide is not considered by parents, teachers, and the community at large, then a child may be severely injured or die, and many people may be adversely affected. A successfully completed suicide attempt leaves enormous devastation in its wake for families, friends, and the community.

First let us consider the dimension of the problem. Suicide is the third leading cause of death in adolescents aged 15 to 24 (Kaplan & Sadock, 1988). In 1985, 21.4 adolescent boys per 100,000 and 4.4 adolescent girls per 100,000 successfully killed themselves (*Statistical Abstract of the United*

States, 1988). In 1985, 5,121 suicides were reported in this age group (National Center for Health Statistics, 1988), for a combined rate of about 12.9 suicides per 100,000 population. This rate is roughly the same for all ages. These figures represent only those deaths that were identified as suicides. Many others go undetected by family and "experts" and are probably misclassified as accidents. Experts conservatively estimate that between 9,000 and 10,000 adolescents actually kill themselves each year (Curran, 1987). Of course, many more adolescents attempt suicide than actually die of suicide each year. One study that surveyed high school students found that 12.5% of the students reported having made a suicide attempt (Curran, 1987). This is an astounding number, and one wonders if this rate is accurate.

The figures reported above reveal something very important about suicide in this age group: Adolescent boys successfully kill themselves at more than four times the rate of adolescent girls. This fact can obscure another very important one: Although adolescent girls are not as likely as boys to actually kill themselves, they *attempt* suicide about three times more often than boys do. This pattern holds true throughout life, with men completing suicide more often than women, but women being much more likely to attempt it.

Because resistance toward identifying depression and suicide in the under-15 age group is so great, figures for this population are hard to obtain and are probably not very accurate. At any rate, 1.6 boys per 100,000 under 15 were identified as having committed suicide in 1979 compared with 0.5 girls per 100,000 (Eisenberg, 1984). This represents a threefold increase of suicides reported in this group since 1950 (Eisenberg, 1984). It is unclear whether this represents a true increase or better identification and reporting. In 1985, 278 children between the ages of 5 and 14 were identified as having killed themselves (National Center for Health Statistics, 1988); just as the reported numbers are probably lower than the actual figures for adolescents, this number is probably also an underrepresentation of actual suicides. It has been conservatively estimated that about 1,000 children under 15 actually commit suicide each year.

Another important fact about suicide is that most successful suicides are preceded by one or more unsuccessful attempts. It is rare for someone to succeed at suicide on the first attempt, although males are more likely than females to do so. The vast majority of people who attempt suicide never actually kill themselves, but they do suffer significant illness and, sometimes, disability from their attempts. It is estimated that from 16 to 200 attempts at suicide occur for every completed suicide, most of which are never recognized as suicide attempts.

Methods of suicide and attempts vary by age and sex. Younger children tend to try methods that are much less lethal than older children and adults. The five most common methods for young children are jumping from heights, self-poisoning, hanging, stabbing, and running into traffic (Pfeffer, 1984).

The likelihood that a child has ingested a poisonous substance by accident decreases with increasing age. In fact, ingestion of a poison in a child over the age of 6 should be considered a suicide or homicide attempt until proven otherwise. Older children and adolescents are much better judges of what is likely to be harmful, and they tend to favor overdose on medication as their method. Males generally tend to choose more violent methods than females. For example, males are much more likely than females to shoot or hang themselves, which may explain their higher rate of successful suicides.

It is often said that children and especially adolescents make suicide threats to manipulate parents, teachers, and friends. It is true that many suicide attempts are not terribly serious, and the individuals involved are fairly certain that they will not die from the attempt. However, this does not mean that these suicide threats and "gestures" are benign and can be ignored. Children and adolescents who threaten suicide and make these gestures desperately need attention. They may feel trapped and not understand how to ask for help in more appropriate ways. They may have tried to ask for help appropriately, but not have been heard by the adults around them. They may feel that the adults are unable or unwilling to respond to their needs, and so they attempt suicide as a means to get others involved in their care. In this sense, suicide threats and gestures *are* manipulations.

If we do not intervene in *appropriate* ways, these "manipulations" can escalate into more serious suicide attempts and ultimately into injury or death. Although we cannot allow ourselves to be manipulated into taking a particular action by a young person's threat of suicide, we must listen to the real plea behind the threat and take action based on the reality of the situation. For example, the boy who threatens to kill himself if his girlfriend breaks up with him is telling us something important about himself. There are two possibilities here. One is that this threat is pure deception and he has no remote intention of harming himself. He just wants to make his girlfriend do what he wants, and he has learned that playing upon other people's guilt is sometimes effective. The other possibility is that this boy has such low self-esteem that he cannot tolerate the idea of losing his girlfriend. He may be quite depressed. He threatens suicide because he is desperate. Both these situations require action that has nothing to do with whether the girlfriend breaks up with him. In both cases the real motives for the threat of suicide need to be investigated. Truly manipulative individuals need to be confronted about their behavior. Depressed individuals need other interventions. Both types of individuals may need professional evaluation and treatment. But until we know exactly what the case is, we take great risk assuming that the behavior is not intended seriously.

Any child or adolescent who *repeatedly* tries to manipulate by means of suicidal threats or gestures is in need of intervention. It is also quite probable that the family needs intervention. Manipulative negative behaviors do not persist unless there is some kind of payoff. Without realizing it, families can become entrenched in patterns of response to these threats that ensure their continuance. Most children do not think to threaten suicide unless they are feeling hopeless and suicidal or they have observed someone else, usually a family member, use these threats to manipulate others. Although it is tempting to dismiss some suicidal threats and gestures because there is an element of manipulation to them, it is very unwise to do so. In actuality, most suicide threats and attempts contain elements of both manipulation and desperation. Although depression may not be the underlying problem, another severe problem is present and should be dealt with. Even manipulations can lead to injury and death in this area of human behavior. The key here is *appropriate response*, which is discussed later. But before we can respond, we need to know how to identify those at risk.

Risk Factors

Who are these children and adolescents who attempt suicide? What are the risk factors, signs, and symptoms that can help us identify them? First, children and adolescents who attempt suicide are usually depressed, and all the clues we use to help us identify depressed children can alert us to the possibility of suicide. (Refer to Appendix B for risk factors and other signs of depression.) However, not all depressed children are at the same risk. There are children at more risk, and times of increased risk for some children. Among children and adolescents who are depressed, those who are more irritable, more easily hurt, more easily angered, more easily frustrated, and more impulsive than other depressed individuals are at increased risk.

The most serious depressions correlate somewhat with increased risk for suicide, but many other factors should be considered. For example, the most extremely depressed people are usually so ill that they do not eat, get out of bed, talk, or even move around much. These individuals have so little energy and are so apathetic that they cannot even muster the motivation it takes to make and carry out a suicide plan. They *are* at risk, however, of starving to death. As people who are very severely depressed get treatment and begin to feel better, many of them actually go through a period (as they are improving) of increased suicide risk. This occurs because as hopeless, demoralized individuals begin to regain energy and take charge of their lives, they sometimes get motivated enough to solve the problem in a final way through suicide. For children and adolescents, this dangerous time should be spent in a hospital. Luckily, this type of depression is rare in very young children.

As mentioned previously, depressed children who have close family members or friends who have died by suicide are at especially high risk to attempt suicide themselves. Even if family members or friends have unsuccessfully attempted suicide, the children also may be at increased risk to attempt suicide. This increased risk seems to remain in effect throughout life. We must remember that adults are role models for children, and if an adult attempts suicide (especially repeatedly), then the child may see this as an acceptable solution to problems encountered in life. Children who have previously attempted suicide are at increased risk to try again and should be closely monitored if still depressed. Having tried to harm oneself once somehow makes it easier to try again. If the attempt is recognized by adults and the underlying causes addressed, the child is less likely to repeat the behavior. Unless the problems that led to the first attempt have been at least partly solved, the child is at risk to try again. Hope appears to be the real key; when children feel that their problems have been taken seriously and real changes have been made to help them, then they are less likely to try again.

Children who threaten suicide or who talk about suicide only in relation to other people are at increased risk. Many studies have verified that most children and adolescents who attempt suicide have told others of their desire and plans ahead of time. Most of them have seen a health professional within a few months of the attempt, but their depression and distress go unrecognized. Teachers and parents, indeed anyone who has regular contact with children and adolescents, must be on the lookout for the signs and symptoms of depression and must listen for talk of suicide.

Physical and sexual abuse also place children and adolescents at greater risk to attempt suicide. Many of these individuals are quite depressed because of the demoralizing and hopeless situation in which they find themselves, and, being immature, they do not see other realistic means of escape. If all you have known all your life is pain and suffering, what cause do you have to believe that life could possibly be any different? Under these circumstances, suicide appears almost reasonable. Most of these children somehow struggle through their childhood, only to find themselves, as adults, repeating the patterns with their own children or repeatedly choosing partners who continue to abuse them.

Those children who drink alcohol and/or take street drugs are also at higher risk. These agents lessen normal inhibitions and increase impulsivity, thereby increasing the risk for suicidal behavior. A very high proportion of suicide attempts are initiated while under the influence of alcohol and other drugs in adolescents and adults. It is quite probable that a significant number of "accidents" that occur to drunk or "stoned" individuals are not accidents at all, but impulsive suicide attempts. A good example of this is the quiet teenage boy who gets drunk, loses control of his car, and is killed when the car hits an abutment. There is no way to know for sure if this particular incident is a suicide, but experts are certain that many "accidents" are in fact suicides. Even minor setbacks, disappointments, and losses can trigger impulsive suicide attempts if the person is under the influence of a mind-altering drug.

Chronic illnesses of all kinds are also linked to suicide attempts and depression. Chronic emotional and behavioral problems other than depression are a special risk factor. Conduct disorders, drug abuse, eating disorders, and certain kinds of personality problems are frequently associated with suicide. In conduct disorders and personality disorders, there is a chronic pattern of negative behaviors that sometimes include repeated suicide threats and attempts. In drug abuse disorders, cocaine addicts are prone to very serious paranoia and depression upon withdrawal of the drug. This sometimes leads to suicide attempts. PCP (angel dust) is also notorious for making people very impulsive and occasionally very paranoid and suicidal.

Children and adolescents diagnosed as having a serious mental disorder such as schizophrenia or mania are at especially high risk. It is not uncommon for schizophrenic children or teenagers to hear voices (auditory hallucinations) that tell them they are worthless and to kill themselves (command hallucinations). These command hallucinations are very dangerous, because the ill person sometimes carries out the instructions and attempts suicide. In mania (which is like the opposite of depression), the person feels very "high" or is very hostile or very irritable. People with this disorder, including those under 18, have decreased inhibitions and are very impulsive. They frequently do very foolish things while in this state (including harming themselves). Sometimes when they are back to normal they become so upset with their former behavior that they try to harm themsleves. In young people with these serious illnesses, those who are more intelligent may be at even higher risk. It seems that those who are able to understand the serious implications of these illnesses and their potential to disrupt lives are more apt to feel hopeless and demoralized by their condition.

Successful suicide depends upon the availability of suitable lethal means to carry it out. For this reason, the presence of guns and ammunition in the home is very dangerous and increases the risk to children and adults. Because suicide (and homicide for that matter) is often an impulsive act, it is best that there be no easy access to guns. Most of the means by which people try to harm themselves take time to be effective. This fortunate circumstance allows us to rescue the victim and prevent suicide. Firearms are all too often quickly effective in their work. It is wise to have no guns in homes where depressed, impulsive, or immature individuals (i.e., children) live.

Times of Greatest Risk

A recent death in a family or among friends from any cause marks a time of increased risk for already depressed children. Some children and adolescents may try to join the deceased in the hereafter if their environment does not contain other people to whom they are strongly and positively attached. This is most likely to occur if the child perceives the dead person as the only one who loved and cared for him or her. Suicide can also be attempted by individuals who did not appear at all depressed prior to the death of their loved one. In this case, the act is probably an impulsive one that may have been initiated while under the influence of drugs or alcohol.

A public humiliation or even the threat of one as perceived by an adolescent or child is also an immediate risk factor for suicide attempts. It does not matter that a teacher or parent does not perceive the event as humiliating or embarrassing. What matters is how the child perceives it. For example, the perfectionist teenage honor student, president of the student council, captain of the basketball team, boyfriend to the prettiest cheerleader, who feels excessive pressure from parents to succeed in everything, may attempt suicide if he missed that winning basket the whole team was counting on. He may attempt suicide if his girlfriend tries to break up with him. He may even attempt suicide if he flunks just one exam. Of course, not every successful student is in danger of committing suicide over one minor failure. The clue to those in danger lies in how important absolute perfection is to the individual involved and how low his or her general self-esteem is.

It is becoming well known to law enforcement officials that young male suspects from good families with no previous records who are jailed for minor offenses awaiting arraignment or bail are at very high risk of killing themselves in their cells. Whether they have actually committed a crime of any sort as ascertained later may not even be related to the suicide attempt. It is the humiliation of being incarcerated and the mistakenly perceived desperateness of their situation that seems to precipitate these suicides.

All too often we read in the paper of a person, usually an adult, but occasionally an adolescent or rarely a child, who suddenly murders several people and then kills himself or herself. These people are almost without exception very disturbed and very depressed. Frequently, the timing of the murders and suicide is related to an upcoming public exposure of some serious crime or indiscretion on the part of the murderer / suicide victim. The majority of the time the individuals murdered are members of the suicide's family, and he or she has killed them either to stop the exposure or to spare them the pain his or her exposure will cause them. The murderer / victim sees the family as an extension of himself or herself and so suicide may include them.

If there has been a recent well-publicized suicide of a child in the local community, other depressed children of similar age and circumstance may be at increased risk even if they do not know the person involved. It appears that the successful suicide of a nearby person lessens the inhibitions that keep some people from attempting suicide. It is almost as if the person thinks, "If they can do it, then I can do it, too. It's not too horrible, hard, messy, painful," and so on. The appropriate reporting of successful child and teenage suicides is a subject of intense scrutiny because of several suicide epidemics following reports in the media. It is important for the general public to be aware of the ever-increasing problem of suicide in our culture, but it is also important to prevent those that we can. (See Appendix C for a summary of the risk factors for suicide.)

Signs of an Impending Suicide Attempt

Beware children who begin to talk about the future in terms that show they do not expect to be a part of it. Children who say goodbye in final terms and who talk matter-of-factly about when they are gone may have planned suicide for the very near future. If these children have spoken of suicide directly in the past but do not directly mention it now, they are probably at extreme risk. People most intent on actually killing themselves will choose times and locations that minimize the probability of rescue. Clues to these planned events do exist, but we must be very conscientious to look for them.

The very depressed child or adolescent who suddenly brightens and appears very relaxed and carefree for the first time in a long while is at extreme risk for a successful suicide attempt in the very near future. Many children and adults contemplate suicide for long periods of time. As part of their depression, they see themselves as very unworthy individuals who only cause pain and suffering to themselves and those they love. Every day is renewed agony for them. When these individuals finally make a decision to kill themselves and formulate the plan to carry it out, they many times feel as if a great burden has been lifted from them. They feel that they have finally found the solution to the misery they cause, and, consequently, they are relieved and relaxed as they await the right time to carry out their plan. *These individuals need immediate intervention.*

Take heed of children or adolescents who begin to give away all of their possessions, especially the most beloved toys or personal articles. Many times just prior to a very serious suicide attempt, individuals will "put their affairs in order." To children and adolescents this usually means finding new homes for all their prized possessions. They may also make global statements of apology to family and friends for past misdeeds or imagined slights of others. They may attempt to set everything in their life aright so that all "debts" are paid if only for a brief time prior to their planned death. Again, *these children and adolescents need immediate intervention.* They are at extreme risk for a serious suicide attempt.

Because suicide attempts so often go unrecognized, it seems wise at this point to include a discussion of signs and symptoms. Three such events that were overlooked and are typical of these incidents were presented in Chapter 1. It is important to recognize suicide attempts even long after the fact because they predispose to more attempts. Recognition could save a child's life. Hindsight in these cases is infinitely better than no sight.

The Accident That's Not an Accident

In the first vignette described in Chapter 1, "Bobby" chose the most common method of suicide used by young children to attempt suicide: He leaped from the jungle gym. Jumping from heights is a method open to even very young children. Several risk factors and signs of depression as discussed in the section on depression are present in this case. He acts "bad" at school (because he feels "bad" on the inside and has low self-esteem), has poor academic performance (because his concentration is very poor, he is unmotivated, and feels no pleasure in succeeding at school), and lives with a chronically ill father (chronic family stress).

A young girl purposely falls while turning a cartwheel with the intention of harming herself. Both of these represent unrecognized attempts on the part of these children to harm themselves. Although it is pretty obvious that these events were not likely to kill the children involved, they are serious episodes. If the child feels that the behavior is likely to be harmful and pursues it, then we must take it seriously. It is the intent of the child that is the determining factor.

All "accidents" suffered by children and adolescents should be scrutinized carefully for the possibility of suicidal intent. The child who falls off a jungle gym or out of a tree, the child who was hit by a car while crossing the street or riding his or her bike, the adolescent who has a one-car accident because he or she "lost control" of the car, or the teenager who cut himself or herself severely while using a large knife in the kitchen are all examples of children who may have had suicidal intent. We must not assume that things are always as they appear or even as they are explained away by the children and adolescents involved. If other signs and symptoms of depression are evident, further inquiry is required.

Accident-proneness is a special characteristic of some children that occasionally turns out to be suicidal in nature. If any of the above examples or other similar events happen repeatedly to a child or adolescent, then there is definitely a problem. Depression and overt or even unconscious suicide intent may be present. Or a medical condition impairing perception or coordination and requiring treatment may be present. Either way, these children need to be evaluated and a cause sought. The possibility of suicide attempts must not be overlooked.

Unconscious suicidal attempts or intent as mentioned above require some explanation. We all know of people who seem bent on self-destruction by smoking in the face of lung cancer, drinking and driving repeatedly, or living in such a way that they constantly place their lives in danger. These people are frequently depressed and their behavior is suicidal in a way, although not necessarily in an immediate sense. This self-destructive behavior of a more insidious and global nature should also be taken as a possible sign of depression. If one were to question these people, chances are that they would deny the suicidal intent of their behavior, and that is what marks it as unconscious. We can, however, think of these behaviors as unrecognized suicide attempts. If such behavior appears in a child or adolescent, it warrants immediate investigation.

"Tiffany" of the second vignette in Chapter 1 is an extremely young example of purposeful overdose on medication. This composite illustrates several important risk factors for suicide. The mother in this example has serious mental illness with probable depression, and the young child witnesses a suicide attempt. Also, this child may have thought her mother was dead and so tried to kill herself in an attempt to join the mother in the hereafter. Incidents of this sort are often treated as accidental poisonings at the time they occur, and without intervention the child may go on to make other serious suicide attempts.

Children and teenagers who "accidentally" take too much of their prescription medication may be suicidal. Teenagers, such as those who take medication for seizures or recent injury or infection, need supervision from an adult. If they are given responsibility for taking the medication themselves, an adult should periodically check the number of pills or capsules left to make sure the amount tallies with what should be left. Depressed adolescents should probably not be left in charge of their own medication. The risk of suicide is present, and depressed individuals frequently have decreased concentration which can lead to missed doses or doubled doses. Depending upon the medication, either can be harmful.

Do not be misled by adolescents who tell you that they dropped the bottle and spilled the contents or that they lost the medication or the prescription before it was filled. These events can mask the hoarding of pills prior to an attempt or cover up after the fact. Did this child appear very sleepy or ill recently? Remember to keep track of your own medication also. Are the number of pills in the bottle the amount you thought you had? The third vignette describing "Frank" is a good case in point. When observing his sleepy behavior, many people would postulate drug abuse as a possible cause. We are doing a much better job of educating ourselves about the drug problem in this country, but we are still ignoring suicide and depression. A suicide attempt with a family member's prescription tranquilizer can be easily mistaken for drunkenness at school. Parents frequently assume that the adolescent is trying to get high and do not take him or her to an emergency room after an overdose. Whenever a child or adolescent appears inappropriately sleepy or drunk at home or school, we need to investigate the possibility of both drug abuse and suicidal intent.

CHAPTER 5

What Can I Do?

A STEP-BY-STEP APPROACH TO DEALING with depressed or suicidal young people is outlined in this chapter. Practical information about initiating intervention and seeking treatment is offered to concerned adults.

How to Get Started

Now that you have learned the signs, symptoms, and risk factors for depression, what do you do if you think you know a child or adolescent who might be depressed? Any child you are worried about should be observed carefully. Go over the material just covered and jot down all the characteristics listed that you have noted in this child. If you have listed more than a couple of the signs or symptoms of depression, then this child may be depressed. Look at the family risk factors, see if any of these are present in this child, and jot them down. If one or more of these are present, then there is a good possibility that this child may be depressed or have some other problem that warrants further investigation.

The next step is to approach the child if you are in a position to do so (e.g., if you are the parent or a teacher of this child). Try to find a quiet time when you are unlikely to be interrupted. It is best if you are in a place where others are unlikely to overhear what is said. The timing should be such that you have not had a negative interaction with this child. The setting should be relaxed and open-ended. Performing a pleasant task together may provide a good setting as long as the task is not a particularly demanding one. Parents will have more chances to create such times than teachers will, but both can manage to do so with a little creativity.

It is frequently a good idea to broach the subject with an observation that you have made. For example, "Susan, I've noticed you look tired a lot these days," or, "Ben, I've noticed that you seem to get angry easily these days," or, "Alison, you seem to be having more difficulty at school than you used to," would be reasonable opening statements. Always try to phrase the observation in as neutral a way as possible. Using the word *seem* has some advantages because it implies that you realize your statement is just an interpretation and not a pronouncement. Adolescents in particular may take umbrage if they think that you assume you know what is going on with them. The idea is to let children know that you have noticed something about their behavior, that you are not looking for faults in their personality, and that you are genuinely concerned about them.

The next step is to wait and see if there is a response to your observation. Some children and adolescents will immediately respond to this with a confirmation of what you have noticed: "Yeah, I just don't have any energy anymore," or, "I try real hard and everything just seems to go wrong these days." Self-revealing statements such as these two should be followed by a supportive comment on your part and perhaps an inquiry into what may be happening in their lives that is contributing to their feeling this way: "That must be hard for you. Do you have any ideas about what might be causing it?" If you get a response to this, then you are off and running with a good beginning.

A youngster with whom you have established a good rapport can be asked more direct questions about his or her feelings. However, remember that most children, and especially very young children, will not identify the way they feel as being "depressed." Other expressions should also be used when questioning them. "Do you feel 'down in the dumps?' " is a good example. Other expressions that commonly refer to a depressed mood in the vernacular are, "low," "blue," "empty on the inside," "down," "sad," "unhappy," and "bad feeling on the inside." All of these can be used when questioning children about how they feel.

What about children who do not respond to your observations about their behavior? After waiting a moment, it is reasonable to inquire into their feelings in a very supportive manner: "I was wondering if maybe you are not feeling well or if maybe something was going on to make things more difficult for you?" This type of inquiry will start a few more children and adolescents talking. Some will respond to this by bursting into tears if they are depressed and barely coping. Some will deny that anything is wrong and will vehemently challenge your original observation: "Nothing's going on. I don't know what makes you think that. I'm not tired at all!" The more strongly they deny your mild observation and question, the more likely it is that something is going on. However, do not force the issue at this point.

In talking with children and adolescents about feelings, it is best to follow their lead. Even if you are unable to get a discussion going at this point, you have at least planted the seed that you have noticed their distress and that you care. Children and adolescents who are reacting negatively to what you are saying still may hear your concern, especially if you do not press them and are nonjudgmental in your approach. Avoid making statements that are black and white and presume to know what this person may be feeling. Avoid "should"-type questions and statements. They tend to make people who are depressed feel guilty and hence more depressed. Avoid asking questions using the word *why,* as it tends to put people on the defensive and most children have difficulty conceptualizing the causes of their distress. Trying to answer such questions may distress them even more. Instead, invite them to speculate on changes they have gone through and how these might be related to how they are feeling.

Listening attentively is one of the most important things you can give any child or adolescent. Taking their feelings, ideas, and problems seriously shows that you respect them as individuals. A child or teen who feels respected is more able to talk about personal matters. Stifle your desire to give advice and avoid a condescending or parental tone. If your attempts fail at this time, invite the individual to talk to you another time if a problem comes up. Then create more quiet, pleasant times with this person to provide an appropriate, conducive atmosphere.

Parents who are worried about their children may elect at this point to talk with school personnel to see if any unusual behaviors have been noted at school. The child may have expressed distress to a trusted teacher. After you notify the child or teen, you may question other relatives and close friends as to whether anything has been noted. Friends may volunteer that they have been very concerned about your child or that your child has made suicidal statements to them.

But what if you are not the parent? Teachers and others involved with children and adolescents may be very worried about depression or suicide in some youngsters they know. If a child or teen does confide in you, what is the next step? If you have approached a teen or child, but he or she has not responded to your inquiry, what is the next step? If you are seriously worried that a child may be depressed or suicidal, it is your ethical and moral responsibility to notify a parent or guardian. Keep in mind that when a child's life or health is in danger, preservation of life or health takes precedence over confidentiality.

The notes made earlier of signs and symptoms in the child should come in handy when you talk with the parent or guardian. Share your observations and concerns, preferably in person. As in dealing with the youngster, try to present your observations in as neutral and supportive a way as possible. "I have noticed that your child is quite tearful and upset at school. Is everything going OK at home?" As in dealing with the child, wait for a response before proceeding. Some parents will recount the problems at home at this point, others will mildly deny an awareness of anything amiss, and still others may vehemently deny any problems and accuse you of meddling.

The worried parent can be referred to his or her own pediatrician or family doctor at this point for initial evaluation of the problem. School counselors may be involved in helping to understand the problem and deal with the school dysfunction it engenders. Parents should be praised and supported in their attempts to find answers to the questions their child's behavioral and emotional state presents.

Through a series of meetings, the unaware or uninterested parent can gradually be encouraged to take the problem seriously if the child's behavior does not improve over a few weeks. The teacher can continue to make himself or herself available to the student in case the student wishes to talk. If serious problems are uncovered during these talks, then the teacher can notify the school counselor and/or school administration if the parent remains unconcerned. Serious untreated emotional and behavioral problems, just like physical ones, require that the school take a firm stance with parents regarding intervention. Requiring a physician's or other professional's note for readmittance to school can force reluctant parents or parents in denial to seek help for the child.

Many schools have access to psychologists who can do evaluations. When evaluations done by school confirm serious depression or suicidal ideation, parents should be encouraged to take appropriate action for further evaluation and treatment for continued school attendance. Because most communities have access to public mental health clinics, lack of funds is not sufficient justification for parents to ignore these problems. Failure to attend to a documented mental health problem of a youngster constitutes neglect; this should be explained to parents.

The resistant parent who denies that anything is wrong in spite of clear evidence to the contrary is naturally very frustrating to teachers and others who want to help a distressed youngster. Realistically, there will be times when there is nothing you can do to get help for a child. If possible, try to refrain from making these parents feel you are against them. Try to be helpful in order to at least maintain a dialogue with the resistant parent. Most parents in this category are themselves very distressed on some level. By remaining supportive and helpful, there is the possibility that at some point in the future you may be able to break through the resistance and enlist these parents' aid in helping their child.

How to Bring Up the Subject of Suicide

All children whom we suspect are depressed should be asked about suicidal thoughts and actions. Many people are under the mistaken notion that to ask about such things directly is dangerous. This is a very harmful myth. There is no evidence to support the idea that if we bring the subject up, we will cause the child to contemplate it at that point. Children who have not thought about suicide usually think it is a silly question and then just forget about it. Youngsters who have contemplated suicide are usually very much relieved that you have asked and respect you for having taken them seriously.

So how does one ask such a question? You can launch into this line of questioning right after asking about depressed feelings, as previously discussed. For example, if a child responds to the question, "Do you feel blue?" (or "down" or "low") affirmatively, you can immediately follow this up with a question about suicidal thoughts. "Have you ever felt so blue (or 'down' or 'low,' etc.) that you didn't want to live anymore?" If the answer is yes, then ask the child to tell you about when he or she had those thoughts. Other follow-up questions should also be asked: "Did you think about harming yourself?" "Do you think about dying?" "Have you ever tried to hurt yourself?" "What ways did you try or think about trying?"

When Immediate Action Is Necessary

There are times when immediate action by parents and teachers is necessary to protect a child. Children who indicate they think about hurting themselves or dying need immediate evaluation and intervention by a competent professional. Children who are suspected of suicidal thoughts or tendencies likewise need immediate intervention. Only a trained professional should be in the position of determining the seriousness of suicidal thoughts and the potential for suicide attempt.

Parents should arrange an emergency evaluation for an actively suicidal child with one of the professionals listed in the next section. It is preferable to contact a physician in case hospitalization is necessary. Children at high risk or those suspected of suicidal tendencies should be evaluated with little time delay. How to find a professional is discussed in the next section.

School officials should contact the parents of any child exhibiting self-injurious behavior (or intent to harm the self) at school and should require intervention prior to returning to school. Ideally, schools should maintain a list of appropriate professionals to whom to refer emergency evaluations. Most parents will have trouble finding an appropriate person on short notice and will welcome this information. A prior relationship between schools and referral mental health professionals or agencies can smooth the way for anxious parents of suicidal and depressed youngsters.

In the course of talking with depressed or otherwise distressed youngsters, teachers may become aware of the occurrence of physical or sexual abuse involving the youngster. This circumstance also requires immediate intervention as it must, by law in most states, be reported to child welfare authorities. Laws vary somewhat as to who must report and the procedure to follow, but those who deal with children have a moral obligation to intervene in these circumstances. This is in the best interests of the child, as no effective treatment for depression and/or suicidal tendencies can take place in the context of ongoing abuse.

The Next Step—Seeking Help

Teachers and school officials can use the following as a guide to help worried parents who have a depressed or behaviorally or emotionally disturbed child and who wonder what to do. The next step for worried parents is to make an appointment with the family doctor or pediatrician. A physical checkup is in order, along with a discussion of concerns. Make sure the doctor is aware of the behaviors and changes that have been noted. The illness of depression is primarily diagnosed on the basis of a normal physical exam, normal laboratory tests, and the characteristic history of signs and symptoms. After physical factors have been investigated and ruled out by the doctor, a referral to a professional specializing in child and adolescent mental health is in order.

Types of Mental Health Professionals

Mental health professionals come in many varieties reflecting a diversity of backgrounds and training. It is important to be careful when choosing one, because many are not trained specifically in diagnosing and treating emotional/behavioral problems in children and adolescents. This point is particularly important in the evaluation of depression in children, because until recently these problems were not even recognized as occurring in children. Many otherwise competent child specialists are still inexperienced in this area. Some may be very competent in evaluating adult emotional and mental health problems but be quite inadequate when dealing with the younger set. The more training and experience the professional has that relates specifically to children and adolescents, the more likely the evaluation will be reliable and useful. The following is a brief guide to the types of professionals and their training.

Psychiatrist. A psychiatrist is a physician with 4 years of training after medical school in the diagnosis and treatment of mental disorders. Rarely do general psychiatrists have more than 3 to 6 months' specialized training in child and adolescent mental health problems. Total length of training is generally 8 years, excluding college.

Child Psychiatrist. A child psychiatrist is a physician with 5 or 6 years of training after medical school in the field of mental disorders. Two of these years are devoted exclusively to diagnosis and treatment of childhood and adolescent mental and behavioral problems. Total length of training is generally 9 or 10 years, excluding college.

Psychologist. Licensed psychologists usually hold a doctoral degree in psychology. They have generally completed 2 years of hands-on training with clients (1 year practicum and 1 year internship) in addition to coursework to earn the degree. Psychologists receive specific training to administer and interpret psychological tests. Total length of training, excluding college, is approximately 4 or 5 years. Please note that training for psychologists may be less standardized than that for psychiatrists, and it may be wise to inquire about their training and experience in diagnosing and treating depressed youngsters before seeking services.

Child Psychologist. This professional is one who concentrated upon working with children during the 2 years of hands-on training. Child psychologists should be trained to administer tests that delineate personality and emotional traits and problems.

Educational Psychologist. Educational psychologists are professionals who concentrated upon working with children in the school setting during the 2 years of practical training. They are trained to do the types of testing useful to schools.

Counseling Psychologist. These professionals are trained in counseling during the 2 years of practical work with clients. The exact nature of training may vary. Some are trained to administer psychological tests.

Social Worker. The social worker usually has a masters degree (2 years or more past college). Training varies enormously. Inquiry should be made about whether formal training and experience with depressed youngsters is part of the professional's background. Social workers are not trained to formally diagnose or administer psychological tests. Some are trained to do psychotherapy or counseling with emotionally disturbed youngsters and their families.

Choosing the Appropriate Professional

Each of these professionals has advantages and disadvantages, mostly relating to intensity of training and cost. The most specialized, comprehensive, and therefore expensive services are likely to be provided by child psychiatrists and clinical child psychologists. Child psychiatrists are physicians who can hospitalize and prescribe medication, if necessary. They are, unfortunately, in short supply in many areas, and a child-oriented psychologist may be more available. Whatever professional you choose to evaluate your child, it is important to find out his or her experience and credentials as they relate specifically to children and adolescents. As an informed consumer, you will be in a better position to make decisions for and with your child.

Many parents will be referred to a psychiatrist, psychologist, or other mental health professional by their pediatrician or family doctor. Even in this case, it is wise to inquire into the experience and training of this person prior to going for an evaluation. Information pertaining to professional training and experience should be available from the referring physician and by telephone from the professional's office. Beware of anyone not willing to discuss this simple information over the phone. If there are any doubts, this information can usually be verified by the local medical society for a physician and by the respective state licensing boards for physicians, psychologists, and other mental health professionals. Practitioners who are not required to obtain state licenses to practice may not be worthy of your consideration.

In the event that a referral from a trusted physician is not available, there are other ways to locate qualified professionals. If you are fortunate to be near a medical school, a call to the school's department of psychiatry should quickly result in a reliable referral. Most medical schools will run their own child mental health clinic staffed with a multispecialty treatment team composed of psychiatrists, psychologists, and social workers. Their services are likely to be very comprehensive, reliable, and competitively priced. Most of these clinics also have a sliding scale fee system based on income.

If you are not located near a medical school, a call to the American Academy of Child and Adolescent Psychiatry should identify the qualified child psychiatrists nearest to your area. (See Appendix D for the address and telephone number of the academy.) Your telephone book may also have a listing for local public mental health/mental retardation services in your area. These organizations may refer you to a qualified child mental health professional in the private sector. Some areas also have suicide prevention hotlines listed in the local telephone book that can provide reliable referrals for depressed and suicidal youngsters.

Local public mental health clinics are often able to provide these services at reduced cost or on a sliding scale fee based on income. However, you must be careful that the person conducting the evaluation is experienced in child mental health problems. Many of these clinics are underfunded and understaffed and so rely on less qualified individuals. Be sure to ask about credentials and experience.

Many areas also have private not-for-profit child guidance clinics that are able to provide evaluations. These provide a wide range of services and also usually operate on a sliding scale fee based on income. Again be sure to ask about credentials and experience of the person conducting the evaluation. A child psychiatrist and/or child psychologist should be available to conduct the evaluation or provide supervision to the person who does.

As a last resort, you may look in the yellow pages of the local telephone book under the physician specialty headings or the psychologist headings. Also, you may call hospital and county referral services that may be listed in the telephone book. Both of these methods are less than ideal in that there is no control for quality. Telephone listings can be obtained by anyone willing to pay the money, and referral services usually are based on hospital affiliation or paying a fee to be listed. If you use these methods, be sure to ask about credentials, experience, and references prior to making an appointment.

What to Expect from an Evaluation

A properly conducted evaluation of a child or adolescent for depression and/or suicide should consist of inquiry into the following categories:

- Events or observations precipitating the parents to seek evaluation for their child
- Course of child's dysfunction
- Previous interventions by mental health providers, if any
- Child's physical, social, and emotional development to date
- School history
- Drug use or abuse
- Sexual activity
- Previous medical problems and interventions
- Medical and mental health problems in other family members
- Family life including socioeconomic status, ethnicity, religion, family customs and traditions, and so on.

To obtain this complete picture of the child, questionnaires may be used, but the evaluator should interview at least one parent and the child in person. It is always preferable to see both parents and the whole family when evaluating a child or adolescent to obtain the most accurate picture of the problem. Additional information from teachers and close friends is also desirable.

In addition to taking a complete history, the evaluator should see the child or adolescent by himself or herself to conduct a mental status examination and/or clinical interview. This establishes whether the characteristic signs and symptoms of depression are present and detectable the day of the evaluation. Evaluation for possible suicidal thoughts or intent should also take place during this special interview.

A review of the child's physical status should also take place to ascertain if physical disorders mimicking emotional or behavioral problems have been ruled out as possible causes of this child's dysfunction. Practitioners other than physicians are probably not competent to perform this portion of the evaluation. The psychiatrist should review records from the pediatrician's or family doctor's examination and lab work to ascertain the completeness of this evaluation and whether further medical testing is appropriate. If the child has not had a physical examination in the recent past, then one is in order at this point with a physician who has been alerted to the problems being evaluated.

Specialized psychological testing may or may not be recommended after the initial interviews and physical evaluation are complete. Occasionally, further medical testing is advised. These are most appropriate for those occasions when the diagnosis is still in doubt after the evaluation is complete or when other problems are uncovered that confound the evaluation. More rarely, hospitalization may be recommended to complete an evaluation when the problems uncovered are very complex or impossible to unravel on an outpatient basis.

At the end of this process, the parent should be presented with a diagnosis with recommendations for treatment and follow-up. These recommendations and the diagnosis should be thoroughly explained to the parent along with alternatives for carrying out the recommendations. The risks and benefits of any treatment recommended should be discussed, as well as the consequences of electing not to pursue treatment.

What to Expect from Treatment

Treatment for depression may range from a few visits with a therapist to a prolonged stay in the hospital with medication therapy. Intensity of treatment depends upon the severity and causes of the illness. Family involvement in the treatment may also vary depending upon the nature of the depression and the family situation. In most cases parents will be involved in the treatment. Other family members may also be asked to participate.

About Psychotherapy

Psychotherapy, or "talking therapy" as it is sometimes called, is recommended by most professionals for depressed children. For certain mild forms of chronic depression in adults, it has been shown to be equal or superior to all other forms of treatment including medication (Kaplan & Sadock, 1988). For depressions that are mild, have clear precipitating stresses, and are not thought to be biologically based, psychotherapy is probably the treatment of choice for children and adolescents.

Psychotherapy usually consists of one or more sessions per week with the therapist. Length of the session varies from 30 minutes to 50 or 60 minutes. During this time the therapist will invite the child to talk and will practice special techniques to help the child feel supported and understood. Children and occasionally adolescents may engage in play activities with the therapist as another way to get at feelings and important issues. Children and adolescents may act out important ideas in play that they are unable to verbalize directly. It is the therapist's job to decipher the hidden messages in behavior and help the child and parent respond to the content appropriately. It is hoped that gradually the precipitants and confounding factors that initiated and sustain the depression can be unraveled, recognized, and dealt with effectively.

Many parents are uncomfortable with the need for confidentiality in psychotherapy. It is usually explained to the child at the start that everything that they say and do in therapy is private. With a couple of notable exceptions, the parents will not be told what transpires during the sessions. This is to enable children to open up and verbalize what they may perceive as unacceptable emotions and ideas. In the privacy of the therapist's office or playroom, these taboo feelings and ideas can be openly discussed, understood, and worked out by the child without fear of censure or retaliation. This is one of the things that makes the relationship in psychotherapy different from ordinary relationships. Therapy conducted without the assurance of confidentiality is likely to be ineffective.

Confidentiality is not absolute, however. If the therapist has reason to believe the child is in immediate danger, is suicidal, homicidal, or reveals a convincing history of physical or sexual abuse, then parents and other persons will be notified. Confidentiality stops where harm or the intent to harm begins. Occasionally, gray areas arise in the therapy when the child may communicate some information of which the parent should be aware to protect the best interests of the child. In these cases, the therapist will usually negotiate with the child or adolescent and have him or her relate the information directly to the parent. If this attempt is unsuccessful, the therapist may elect to go ahead and tell the parent after first warning the child. These issues usually revolve around drug use, sexual activity, and pregnancy.

Although confidentiality surrounds the content of the psychotherapy sessions themselves, the therapist should communicate with parents on the general status of their child. Feedback and advice is usually given about issues of parenting a depressed or suicidal child. What to expect in the way of changes in the child's behavior as therapy progresses should be discussed. Any questions the parents may have concerning events at home or behaviors they have noted should be communicated to the therapist and discussed.

In addition to individual psychotherapy for the son or daughter, conjoint therapy with parents, child, and sometimes other siblings and family members is occasionally recommended. More rarely it is advised in place of individual psychotherapy for the child. These sessions are used to facilitate increased communication among family members and provide insight into factors stressing the child and family. Negative patterns in the family that reinforce maladaptive behaviors in the child (i.e., vicious cycles) can be identified and strategies to eliminate them formulated. For example, if Suzy feels her parents do not pay much attention to her, she may do obnoxious, negative things to get their attention. The parents may react very strongly to this by telling Suzy she is bad and punishing her. This, of course, gives Suzy lots of attention but also makes her feel more unhappy and unloved by her parents. She may do more obnoxious things out of anger to get more attention. And round and round the cycle goes. In family therapy, these kinds of patterns can be identified and remedied.

About Hospitalization

If the child is noticeably dysfunctional in more than one of the three major spheres of living, hospitalization may be recommended as part of the treatment. Children and adolescents function on the level of the individual, the family, and the community. The child may be very unhappy or miserable, unable to sleep or eat, or actively contemplating suicide; this would constitute considerable dysfunction on the individual level. The child himself or herself is usually quite bothered by the state of affairs. Dysfunction at the family level might consist of severe behavioral problems with which the parents cannot cope. John might be aggressive toward his younger brother in such a way that his health is in danger. Parents might feel unable to leave John with a sitter or alone (if he is an adolescent) because his behavior in the home is so unpredictable. He may be unable or unwilling to follow family rules. Dysfunction in the community might consist of breaking the law, acting out at school, performing far below capacity at school, truancy, or exhibiting any behavior intolerable to the community at large.

Dysfunction in two or three of the above areas makes outpatient work very difficult. So much is going wrong that a couple of hours a week spent in therapy is not going to turn it around. The dysfunctional behaviors have to be under more control before therapeutic work can take place. The hospital supplies a controlled predictable environment where the majority of time is spent in therapeutic interactions. The child is closely monitored and immediately removed from any situation in which he or she is not behaving appropriately.

If the dysfunction in any one life area is sufficiently severe, hospitalization may also be recommended, even if the other two spheres are not problem areas. A good example is the actively suicidal child or adolescent. These children are not necessarily causing any problems in the home or at school for themselves or others. Indeed, they may exhibit exemplary behavior in both places, but if treated on an outpatient basis, a serious suicide attempt may take place. It is very difficult to monitor a child at all times, and most parents are not prepared to do this. The hospital is a wise choice when suicide attempts are a possibility.

Hospitalization should ideally take place at a facility that has a psychiatric unit that specializes in children or adolescents. Young children do best on a unit that does not include adolescents and vice versa. The staff should be trained to work specifically with the age group to which they are assigned. Many communities now have psychiatric hospitals, and many of these do have adolescent units. Special units for younger children are rarer but have been added to many of these hospitals. In addition to private hospitals, most states do have state psychiatric facilities that include specialized units for children and adolescents. Many medical schools also have these specialized units. If hospitalization is recommended for your child, inquire as to the type of hospital and the type of unit on which your child is to be placed. If at all possible, your child should be placed on a specialized unit even if it means he or she is farther from home.

Hospitalization is very stressful for both children and parents. It is not unusual for parents of a hospitalized child to feel great guilt about having a child in the hospital for depression or suicidal tendencies. Many parents say that they feel the hospital staff is blaming them for their children's problems. It is important to remember that this guilt is a natural response and occurs because parents worry about the part they have played in their child's dysfunction. The family therapy and parent meetings that most hospitals include as part of their treatment are designed to help parents deal with these feelings and the reactions to hospitalization. Parents and children should feel free to bring these issues to the attention of the hospital staff during these meetings.

About Medication

Medication is increasingly recommended for both children and adolescents with significant depression. Antidepressants, as these drugs are called, have been shown to be effective in relieving depression in adults for many years. More recently, their effectiveness has been systematically studied in children and adolescents. There is still some controversy among experts as to whether antidepressants should be prescribed in the under-12 age group.

The Food and Drug Administration has not formally approved the use of antidepressant drugs for young children (with one exception, see below), and, for this reason, the most conservative experts do not prescribe them in this age group. FDA approval hinges upon clinical testing of these drugs under very controlled experimental conditions that should show how effective they are and what risks they pose to children. At the present time clinical testing is incomplete and not entirely conclusive. Some antidepressant drugs are already approved for use in teenagers.

Other experts in this field do recommend the use of antidepressants with seriously depressed children. They point out that the studies that have already been completed, although not constituting proof, do strongly suggest both effectiveness and minimal risks with children. From these studies and numerous positive anecdotal reports and empirical observations made by physicians who have used these medicines with children, these experts feel that to withhold antidepressants is not advisable. One of the foremost experts in pediatric psychopharmacology, Joaquin Puig-Antich, goes so far as to say that serious depression is not amenable to other therapies, including psychotherapy, until the depression is first improved with medication (Kaplan & Sadock, 1985).

One antidepressant is already approved for use in children, although not for depression. Imipramine (brand name Tofranil) is an antidepressant drug that has been used for a number of years in children for treatment of chronic bedwetting. This is the medication generally used to treat childhood depression when medicine is recommended. At low doses it is safe and possibly effective. Caution should be exercised when using it at the higher doses needed in treating depression, as it can exert a powerful effect on the heart. If imipramine is used to treat depression, EKGs (examinations of the electrical activity of the heart) are recommended for children about to receive this medication and as treatment progresses.

It should be pointed out that in prescribing a medication that is approved by the FDA for marketing, a physician is not limited by law to the FDA-approved uses or populations. Physicians may appropriately prescribe a drug for a person or a use not included in the official approval if in that physician's professional judgment it is in the best interest of the patient to do so.

In general children actually tolerate most medications better than adults do. Children tend to break medications down and excrete them faster than adults and consequently require proportionately more medicine than adults to produce the same effect. The medicines used to treat depression are no exception. Treated children may need their blood tested to determine if a sufficient amount of the medication is present. To the relief of parents, antidepressants do not produce a "high" of any sort, are therefore not abused, and are not addicting.

If medication is recommended for treating your child or adolescent with depression, your physician should thoroughly discuss with you the rationale for use. The potential risks, benefits, and side effects should be explained to you in detail and your questions answered to your satisfaction. The treatment should be carried out by or under the supervision of a psychiatrist, preferably a child psychiatrist, and the child's progress and reactions carefully monitored. Initiation of such treatment in a young child should probably not take place out of the hospital, although adolescents are sometimes started on these medications as outpatients.

Follow-up of children and adolescents placed on medication is very important to continue to evaluate safety and effectiveness. In children responding well to antidepressants with remission of the signs and symptoms of depression, treatment should last for several months after depression is no longer evident. The medicine should then be gradually reduced and eventually discontinued. Abrupt termination of treatment is not recommended. Although addiction does not take place, the body does make certain compensations because of the presence of these drugs. Discontinuing the medicine all at once can be uncomfortable and/or dangerous for your child.

Whenever a child is placed on any long-term medication, school personnel should be alerted to this fact. Side effects may be present that affect school behavior or performance. Special precautions while the child is at school may be necessary, depending upon which specific medication is prescribed. Adverse reactions may be spotted by a teacher early on in treatment and can then be reported to parent or physician. Teachers and other school personnel can be very valuable allies in monitoring any treatment and determining its effectiveness.

In any person with depression, there are also special precautions that must be taken when medicine is prescribed. Precautions must be taken against the possibility of a suicide attempt with the prescription medication. In the hospital setting, the medication is locked up and meted out to the child only at specified times. Even so, very seriously depressed children have been known to pretend to take their dose, only to save it up over time to use in a suicide attempt. At home, the medicine must be kept in a safe place and its use monitored. The number of pills in the original prescription should be noted, and the amount left in the bottle should reflect appropriate dosing. Parents and school personnel must be aware of the signs of overdose of any medication given to a depressed youngster. Guidelines for administration and information on what to look for in overdose should be supplied by the doctor.

Parents may wish to have on hand one of the current books about medications for the lay public. One such book is *The Essential Guide to Prescription Drugs,* a frequently updated guide written by James W. Long (see Appendix D). These books are very useful, as it is often difficult to remember all the doctor's instructions and information. Having a reliable source of information about the medications for your child is very helpful for the anxious parent of the depressed or otherwise ill child.

Other Therapies

On the horizon are new therapies for depression currently being tested with adults and children. Sleep deprivation and light therapy are two examples. These two therapies are based on studies showing that some people's depressions are related to seasonal variation in available sunlight and the sleep-wake cycle. At present they are promising but experimental. It is unlikely that they will be recommended for your child unless part of a special experimental protocol.

If therapies other than these are recommended for your child or adolescent with depression, scrutinize them carefully. Special diets, megavitamins, and allergy therapy for depression are examples of other types of therapies not generally used in the mainstream practice of psychiatry and psychology. Their status is controversial, and if you embark on a course of treatment for your child that includes one or more of these, please be advised that they are not currently considered proven therapies. Most experts in this field would caution against relying on them as effective treatment for depression. Remember, no course of treatment is completely without risk, and parents must strive to be as informed as possible prior to making important treatment decisions for their children.

A Note About Prevention

The ultimate goal of all professionals dealing with mental health problems is the prevention of these problems in the first place. At the present time, identifying those at risk for depression and suicide prior to the manifestation of the illness and suicide attempts is becoming more precise. Suicide prevention hotlines are available in many areas for telephone counseling and referral of suicidal individuals and those concerned about them. In many instances we assume that suicide is averted because of these programs, but in general the prevention of these problems is in its infancy. The rising rate for suicide and depression in the general public over the past 35 years is an alarming trend that may have our very way of life at its root. The stress of competitive modern life, an environment polluted with toxic chemicals, the spectre of nuclear war, and the breakdown of the extended family unit probably all contribute to some extent. All this makes primary prevention very difficult. Our best hope for the present is early identification of those at risk and immediate therapeutic intervention.

Conclusion

It is hoped that this discussion of depression and suicide in children and adolescents will provoke some second thoughts about youngsters in our midst. Recognizing that the problem exists and becoming aware of its manifestations are absolutely essential if we are to even begin to help those who are suffering. How to recognize potentially depressed children, approach them and their parents, seek help for the problem, and choose appropriate treatment are complex topics that deserve the attention of all who are concerned about the future.

This book is not intended to be an exhaustive source on these topics. As many questions may have been raised as have been answered in these pages. But when we begin to ask questions, we are preparing ourselves to learn, understand, and seek appropriate answers. We hope a place to start has been realized here, along with an indication of the direction to pursue for further information.

A list of the professional references that were used in the preparation of this text is included. While these are not intended for the lay public, they do contain much useful data for those who have questions about anything they have read here. In addition to this, Appendix D is a list of books and organizations that deal with depression, treatment, and parenting for those who wish further information and help.

Appendix A
Signs and Symptoms of Depression in Children

Depressed Mood

Looks sad most of the time
Complains of feeling sad, bad, or tired
Cries easily
Very anxious
Sudden mood changes

Withdrawn

Very quiet
Loses interest in activities
Stays in room most of the time

Poor Concentration

Forgets things
Poor school performance
Trouble finishing chores or homework
Accident-prone

Increased or Decreased Energy

Looks "slowed down" or "speeded up"
Tires easily
Awake at night or very early in morning
Complains of not sleeping
Sleeps all the time
Will not get out of bed

Appetite Changes

Loses or gains weight
Poor appetite
Hungry all the time
Stops growing

Poor Self-Esteem

Unable to tolerate compliments
Makes negative comments about self
Cannot tolerate imperfection in self
"Buys" friends

Suicidal

Talks about death
No goals for future

Any Significant Change in Child

Has many aches and pains
Begins to act more babyish
Uses drugs
Becomes sexually promiscuous

Appendix B
Risk Factors for Depression in Children

Other Family Members with Mental Health Problems

Relatives with depression
Relatives with alcohol problems
Relatives who abuse drugs
Relatives who have been in psychiatric hospital

Important Losses

Death of parent
Death of sibling
Death of other close family
Divorce
Loss of friends because of moving
"Loss" of mother if she returns to work
Death of a pet
Loss of body parts through accident or illness
Loss of important objects
Loss of home

Chronic Stress in Family

Chronic illness in family member
Chronic illness in the child
Loss of parental job with unemployment
Problems with the law

Child Abuse

Physical abuse
Sexual abuse
Emotional abuse

Any Significant Family Change or Stress

Birth of a sibling
Remarriage
Family violence
Parental discord
Suicide in family or friend

Appendix C
Risk Factors for Suicide

Emotional/Behavior Problems

Depression

Impulsive personality
Alcohol abuse
Drug abuse
Other serious psychiatric illness

Decreased Inhibition

Alcohol intoxication
PCP intoxication
Hallucinogen intoxication

Suicide Is Familiar

Suicide threats
Previous suicide attempts
Family member has attempted suicide
Completed suicide in family member
Recent publicized suicide in community

Severe Stress

Recent significant loss
Chronic illness
Public humiliation or threat thereof

Access to Lethal Means

Prescription drugs at hand
Street drugs easy to obtain
Guns and ammunition in home
Has time alone to carry out plan

Remember, girls are much more likely to attempt suicide, but boys are much more likely to succeed.

Appendix D
Resources and Suggested Reading

Sources of Information for Parents and Teachers

American Academy of Child and Adolescent Psychiatry
Virginia Q. Anthony, Executive Director
3615 Wisconsin Avenue, N.W.
Washington, DC 20016
(202) 966-7300

American Psychological Association
Leonard D. Goodstein, PhD, Executive Officer
1200 17th Street, N.W.
Washington, DC 20016
(202) 955-7660

National Alliance for the Mentally Ill
Laurie M. Flynn, Executive Director
1901 North Fort Myer Drive, Suite 500
Arlington, VA 22209-1604
(703) 524-7600

National Depressive and Manic Depressive Association
Marilyn Weiss, President
Merchandise Mart, Box 3395
Chicago, IL 60654
(312) 993-0066

National Institute of Mental Health
5600 Fishers Lane
Rockville, MD 20857
(301) 443-2403

Books on Parenting

Dinkmeyer, D., & McKay, G. (1982). *The parent's handbook: Systematic training for effective parenting (STEP).* Circle Pines, MN: American Guidance Service.

Faber, A., & Mazlish, E. (1980). *How to talk so kids will listen and listen so kids will talk.* New York: Avon.

Gordon, T. (1975). *P.E.T.: Parent Effectiveness Training.* New York: Plume.

Books on Medication

Long, J. W. (1987). *The essential guide to prescription drugs.* New York: Harper & Row.

Griffith, H. W. (1987). *Complete guide to prescription & non-prescription drugs.* Tucson, AZ: HP Books.

References

Beardslee, W. R. (1984). Familial influences in childhood depression. *Pediatric Annals, 13,* 32–36.

Curran, D. K. (1987). *Adolescent suicidal behavior.* Washington, DC: Hemisphere.

Earls, F. (1984). The epidemiology of depression in children and adolescents. *Pediatric Annals, 13,* 23–31.

Eisenberg, L. (1984). The epidemiology of suicide in adolescents. *Pediatric Annals, 13,* 47–54.

Kaplan, H. I., & Sadock, B. J. (1985). *Comprehensive textbook of psychiatry/IV.* Baltimore: Williams & Wilkins.

Kaplan, H. I., & Sadock, B. J. (1988). *Synopsis of psychiatry.* Baltimore: Williams & Wilkins.

Kashani, J. H., Carlson, G. A., Beck, N. C., Hoeper, E. W., Corcoran, C. M., McAllister, J. A., Sallahi, C., Rosenberg, T. K., & Reid, J. C. (1987). Depression, depressive symptoms, and depressed mood among a community sample of adolescents. *American Journal of Psychiatry, 144,* 931–933.

National Center for Health Statistics. (1988). *Vital statistics of the United States, 1985, Vol. II: Mortality.* Washington, DC: U.S. Department of Health and Human Services, Public Health Service, Center for Disease Control.

Pfeffer, C. R. (1984). Clinical aspects of childhood suicidal behavior. *Pediatric Annals, 13,* 56–61.

Saxe, L., Cross, T., & Silverman, N. (1988). Children's mental health: The gap between what we know and what we do. *American Psychologist, 43,* 800–807.

Statistical Abstract of the United States. (1988). Washington, DC: U.S. Department of Commerce, Bureau of the Census.

Webster's new world dictionary (3rd college ed.). (1988). New York: Merriam-Webster.

About the Author

NINA JO MUSE is a physician trained in child psychiatry. After completing her undergraduate degree at Yale University, she received her doctorate in medicine from the University of Texas Medical Branch. General psychiatry training was accomplished under the auspices of the San Mateo County Mental Health Department in California prior to entering the Austin State Hospital Child Psychiatry Program. She directs an inpatient children's psychiatric unit at Charter Lane Hospital in Austin, Texas, and is assistant residency training director of the Austin Psychiatric Residency Program. She wrote this book while taking time off from her career to nurture her first child. Currently, she lives with her impish son, tired pediatrician husband, four fat cats, and one spotted dog in rural central Texas.